709.04014

1387SUX

Art Nouveau Jewellery and Metalwork

Haworth - Maden . Clare (Ed.)

ART NOUVEAU JEWELLERY AND METALWORK

Grange
BOOKS

A QUANTUM BOOK

Published by Grange Books
an imprint of Grange Books Plc
The Grange
Kingsnorth Industrial Estate
Hoo, nr. Rochester
Kent ME3 9ND

1-84013-125-X

This book is produced by
Quantum Books Ltd
6 Blundell Street
London N7 9BH

Project Manager: Rebecca Kingsley
Project Editor: Judith Millidge
Designer: Wayne Humphries
Editor: Clare Haworth-Maden

The material in this publication previously appeared in
*Introduction to the Decorative Arts, Art of Louis Comfort
Tiffany, Encyclopedia of the Decorative Arts, Illustrated
History of Antiques, Encyclopedia of Decorative Styles, Art
of Rene Lalique*

QUMANJM
Set in Times
Reproduced in Singapore by Eray Scan Pte Ltd
Printed in Singapore by Star Standard Industries (Pte) Ltd

CONTENTS

An introduction to Art Nouveau

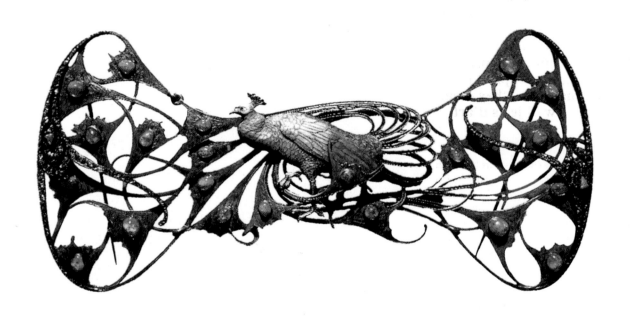

Art Nouveau, which means 'new art', seems an appropriate description for an art movement that bridges the psychological gap between the 19th and 20th centuries. As the 1900s dawned the historicism inspired by the Arts and Crafts Movement began to give way to a new, forward-looking approach. Art Nouveau, which spanned the period roughly from 1895 to 1905, was caught between the joint influences of the old and new and, stylistically, owes something to each. Many designers and craftsmen seeking new sources of inspiration, looked back to earlier times and outwards to exotic cultures and with new methods of production and novel materials, they created exciting new objects d'art.

Far left: A peacock corsage ornament, c.1898-99 in gold, enamel, opals and diamonds by René Lalique.

Below: Wrought iron from the staircase of Horta's Hotel Solvay in Brussels.

SYMBOLISM

One of the major influences on Art Nouveau was the Symbolist movement which had begun in the 1880s in reaction to the optical realism of the Impressionists. The Symbolists sought to depict the 'idea in sensuous form' and, in protest against the increasing industrialisation of society, drew their subject matter from legend, literature, religion and even the occult. Distinguished by a shared attitude rather than a common style – the movement included artists as diverse as Gustav Moreau, Odilon Redon, Puvis de Chevannes, and Ferdinand Khnopff – Symbolist paintings recorded not the observation but the sensation. In both the aim to communicate emotion, and in the subject matter employed to do so, much Symbolist art is closely allied to Art Nouveau: the use of undulating line, the many representations of the nude female figure with, long flowing hair, insects, peacocks, flowers and water-inspired iconography.

The decadent elegance of Symbolism was in many places, to become the hallmark of Art Nouveau: it informs the graphic work of Alphonse Mucha, the glass of Emile Gallé, the jewellery of René Lalique, the ironwork of Hector Guimard and the furniture of Louis Majorelle. But the flowing, flaring asymmetrical lines, and the motifs largely drawn from nature and natural forms employed by Art Nouveau designers were also linked to a variety of different sources.

INFLUENCES FROM ENGLAND

Many of the origins of the Art Nouveau style are to be found also in Victorian England. Here, one discovers not only the sinuous decorative line that was to characterise the appearance of Art Nouveau, but also many of the ideas that were to become its theoretical base.

The Great Exhibition of 1851 held in the Crystal Palace in London's Hyde Park, had been intended not only to demonstrate new technology and promote international trade, but also to advertise what were generally held to be the finest examples of design. The standards of the exhibits on display, however, were to attract a great deal of harsh criticism, from the influential writer and art critic, John Ruskin in particular.

Ruskin hated the mass-produced and shoddily made products that he had seen, and called for a return to craftsmanship. This was largely inspired by a somewhat romantic vision of the Middle Ages through which Ruskin hoped to develop an alternative to the horrors of factory labour and in which he saw as a means of improving the quality of everyday objects.

Above: La Plume calendar by Alphonse Mucha. The jewels recall his work for Fouquet.

Ruskin advised craftsmen and designers to look to nature for their forms and cast off the historical forms common in Victorian revivalism.

MORRIS AND CO.
Ruskin's ideas were taken up by William Morris who as a student had developed a profound affection for the culture of the Middle Ages – not only its architecture, art and craft, but also the artistic co-operation which had fostered their creation. At Oxford, Morris met several others who shared his passion: the architect Philip Webb and the painters Edward

Burne-Jones and Dante Gabriel Rossetti, who were later to become members of the Pre-Raphaelite group.

In his attempt to recreate a medievally-inspired idyll of artists and craftsmen working together on the same tasks, Morris founded a company in 1861 to produce the types of objects he wanted to see in very home. This became Morris and Co. and by employing his Pre-Raphaelite friends to design and decorate furniture, textiles and furnishings, Morris's company was able to produce a complete range of products to furnish a home in a uniform

Above: Cabinet decorated with scenes from the life of St George painted by William Morris. The medievalism of the piece is typical of the furniture produced by Morris & Co during the 1860s.

Right: Christening mug for Lord David Cecil (1902) produced by the Guild of Handicrafts.

style that achieved an overall harmony of effect.

The appearance of the goods made by Morris & Co. was reminiscent of medieval models but the style was also largely derived from natural sources inspired by plant, bird and animal forms. The use of hand-crafted, natural materials, however, inevitably made Morris's goods too expensive for ordinary people, but his example encouraged a number of similar groups of designers to develop. These are generally referred to under the name of the Arts and Crafts Movement.

THE CENTURY GUILD

One of the most important of these enterprises was the Century Guild founded by Arthur Heygate Mackmurdo in 1882. Mackmurdo developed the natural forms that had inspired Morris into elongated, increasingly elegant lines and patterns, and as such, was the first to produce the characteristic vocabulary of Art Nouveau. The new style made its first appearance in the title page design of Mackmurdo's book, *Wren's City Churches,* and the sinuous, rippling pattern of the plants as if they are underwater, were to be the hallmark of the Art Nouveau style for the next two decades.

The theme was rapidly developed by the Century Guild and a number of other bodies such as the Art Worker's Guild founded by Walter Crane and Lewis Day in 1884, and Charles Ashbee's Guild of Handicrafts founded in 1888.

THE GUILD OF HANDICRAFTS

The work produced by the Guild was simple in design. Its metalwork, in the form of jewellery, flatware, plates and vases was, again, often inspired by medieval sources, with the addition of semiprecious stones and decora-

tive devices. Ashbee was one of the first designers in the Arts and Crafts Movement to
experiment in jewellery.

Initially, there were few trained jewellers
involved in the Guild, though many of the
craftsmen involved were experienced metal-
workers in copper and silver. Ashbee's own
designs were in part inspired by the Celtic
Revival which encouraged the use of Celtic
inspired interlaces and coloured enamels, and
in part by the work of Benvenuto Cellini, perhaps the greatest goldsmith of the Italian
Renaissance. To these sources, Ashbee added
motifs of his own and produced a range of
metalwork and jewellery that included covered cups, salvers and ceremonial spoons, and
brooches, buckles, necklaces and even but-
tons decorated with peacocks and flowers, and
enhanced with blue and green enamels and
semiprecious stones.

SPREADING THE STYLE
Public interest grew, largely due to the exhibitions of craftwork organised by the Arts and
Crafts Exhibition Society and the widespread
publicity give to the Arts and Crafts Movement
by art journals such as *The Studio*. The business of Liberty & Co., established in 1875 by
Arthur Lazenby Liberty, modified the handicraft guild's original ideal of solely producing hand crafted goods into another direction
by exploiting both markets and machinery.
Technically, Liberty's factory made commer-
cial products, and although some were hand
finished, they cannot be deemed Arts and
Crafts. Yet many of their designs relate to the
spirit and style of the movement. Liberty &

*Right: A late 19th century silver and
chrysoprase bowl on stand by C.R Ashbee.*

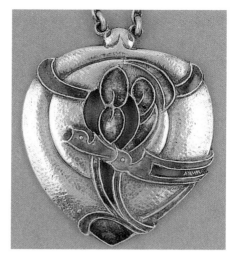

Co. managed to produce and distribute couture, fabrics, furnishings, metalwork, jewellery and furniture to a wider public than either Morris or his followers. Despite the fact that individual handicraft and creative expression often disappeared under Liberty's policy of anonymity for his designers, his employees did include some of the most prominent names in the Arts and Crafts and Art Nouveau design of the time: Charles Voysey, Jessie M. King, Arthur and Rex Silver, Georgina and Arthur Gaskin and Archibald Knox.

ART NOUVEAU ABROAD

This mixture of commerce and art was not restricted to England. The term 'Art Nouveau' itself in fact derives from the Parisian shop of the same name run by a German emigre, Samuel Bing. Bing had been trading for some years in Oriental art and in 1888 had launched a monthly magazine, *Le Japon Artistique*. Japan was a relatively new discovery for the west, haven been opened up to trading by the American Commodore Perry as recently as 1853. Artists such as Gallé, Lalique and Tiffany owed a debt to this 'japonisme'.

The formal links between Japanese art, in particular, Japanese prints and Art Nouveau are strong: the emphasis on decorative line, creating flat, patterned work and the delicate balance between decoration and background were immediately found to by sympathetic. The curving, flowing Japanese line was drawn from observation of nature, filtered

Above: A pendant in enamelled silver by Jessie M. King for Liberty & Co. c.1902.

Right: Print by Hiroshige. The Japanese use of expressive line and a combination of simple flat shapes inspired the painters and designers of late 19th century Europe.

Far right: A lady's sitting room in Bing's Pavillion de l'Art Nouveau, by Georges de Feure, 1900.

through a developed design sense to create more abstract forms and patterns with the precise degree of artificiality that the Art Nouveau artists found so appealing.

LA MAISON DE L'ART NOUVEAU

When he re-launched his shop as La Maison de l'Art Nouveau in 1895, Bing exhibited the work of contemporary designer and artists including Tiffany, Aubrey Beardsley, René Lalique and Emile Gallé. Bing's mixture of gallery and shop was to become the Paris base for the new style of Art Nouveau and his reputation was sufficient for him to be allotted an entire pavilion at the Paris Exposition Universelle of 1900.

International exhibitions throughout the 19th and early 20th centuries became an increasingly important feature of international commerce and in the dissemination of the new style. The depth of interest among the public in new fashions in decorative art were also reflected in a growing number of magazines and periodicals devoted to the new trends.

VARIATIONS ON A THEME

In Germany, the influential Munich-based journal *Jugend* would lend its name to the German version of Art Nouveau, *Jugendstil*. Sometimes here the style was also called '*Studiostil*' after the widely read English, and later American, periodical *The Studio*. In 1907 the *Deutsche Werkbund*, partially inspired by British Arts and Crafts models, was formed by Henry Van de Velde and Hermann Muthesias to promote and alliance between art and industry. The *Werkbund* was not only interested in applying good design principles,

Left: Jugend *magazine, the German journal established in 1896.*

but also in educating the general public to appreciate these principles. Their ultimate goal was to shape the economic and cultural identity of Germany.

AUSTRIA

In Austria the leading organs for Art Nouveau were the periodical *Ver Sacrum* and the members of the *Wiener Werkstätte*. The search for a new style at the beginning of the century was led by Josef Hoffmann and the members of the Secessionist group founded in 1897. The main objective of this group was to improve the status of the decorative arts and in 1903 they established the *Wiener Werkstätte*, a small colony of artists who wished to promote the

Above: A teaset designed by Josef Hoffmann in typical Wiener Werkstatte style. The forms are more traditional than most Art Nouveau ceramics.

Right: A Viking wood carving in an intricate interlaced design.

Far right: A bronze fitting from a Celtic chariot in the form of a horse's head. The combination of stylisation and natural inspiration typified Art Nouveau itself.

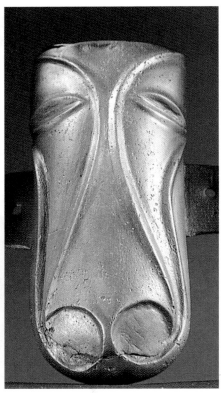

individual creativity of the designer.

NORDIC COUNTRIES

In their search for an aesthetic formula that was in keeping with their cultural traditions, the Nordic countries of Sweden, Denmark, Finland and Norway also drew on the idealised democratic principles of craft production espoused by Ruskin and Morris. Returning to their own indigenous folk art for inspiration, the intricate curves and spirals of this tradition found their way into the local form of Art Nouveau that was even occasionally called the Dragon Style in deference to its Viking sources.

In America, as in England, the Arts and Crafts Movement inspired many individuals to turn to the professional practice of their particular craft. The Arts and Crafts Movement was important in America not only for the fine workmanship it encouraged, but also for the growing awareness it fostered among Americans of the need for a truly national art.

Much of the vitality of Art Nouveau is derived from these and other various centres. Paris and Nancy in France, Munich, Berlin and Darmstadt in Germany, Brussels, Barcelona, Glasgow, Vienna, New York and Chicago were all focal points for a style that was capable of accommodating diversity in regional variations.

ART NOUVEAU
JEWELLERY
IN FRANCE

Above: Pendants in gold and diamonds. Two anonymous examples of Art Nouveau design featuring the 'femme fatale'.

Overleaf: A gold and enamel belt buckle. French, from around 1900.

The standards of French craftsmanship in the area of jewellery were extremely high, and perhaps unrivalled in any other country. In a period rich in its constant variety of invention, the tastes in jewellery were susceptible to the vagaries and whims of fashion, and serve as an expressive mirror of the period, reflecting the hot-house decadence of the fin-de-siècle. In France, Art Nouveau jewellery had its origins in the work of the French goldsmiths whose creations were to become the inspirations for other European craftsmen and women. The most influential among the French artist-jewellers was undoubtedly the glass maker René Lalique.

ART NOUVEAU JEWELLERY

Most characteristic of Art Nouveau is a tendency to asymmetry, producing a sense of instability which is heightened by the use of the whip-lash curves and tendril forms. Another ubiquitous image is of woman, either in the form of the *femme-fleur* (woman as flower) or the dangerous, man devouring, *femme fa-*

18

Left: The more traditional style of jewellery seen in a matching bracelet and pendant from c.1835 in gold, diamonds and garnets.

tale. Much of the imagery in Art Nouveau comes from mythology, whether in the form of winged serpents, the gothic horrors of bats and vampires, or more ethereal creatures, such as peacocks, butterflies and dragonflies.

GOLDSMITHING IN FRANCE
The goldsmith's work that was produced in France, and throughout most of the west be-fore the Art Nouveau period essentially fol-lowed a long established line of classical, baroque and rococo jewellery. It was opulent and ostentatious, and often rather unimagi-native, although one principle that many of the turn-of-the-century goldsmiths did adopt was of the jewel as a miniature work of art. On the whole, goldsmiths generally subjugated whatever innovative talents they might have had in favour of manipulating the precious gems that were at their disposal, namely, the diamond. In the wake of South Africa's 'dia-mond rush' of the 1860s, there was a strong demand for cut diamonds throughout Europe and America, and most goldsmiths tended to work exclusively with these cut stones.

Above: Grasshopper necklace, with horn and pearls, c.1902-04. A popular motif in Art Nouveau, the grasshopper appeared on several Lalique jewels.

viously under-utilised, even scorned 'lesser materials' like glass, horn and tortoiseshell, with rare gems and metals, (such hybrid confections are called 'bijouterie', as distinguished from all-precious 'joaillerie') as well as his use of natural, fantastic, neo-classical and literary images in a sublime way, makes his work an outstanding achievement in the history of Art Nouveau and in the goldsmith's art. Lalique did not forsake precious stones like diamonds, sapphires and topaz altogether, but it was his genius to rediscover semiprecious coloured stones such as opal, chalcedony, agate, jade, chrysoprase and moonstone and to use them in exciting combinations with pearls, translucent, opalescent champlevé and *plique-à-jour* enamels.

LALIQUE'S CAREER

Lalique's background was the perfect blend of art and craft. In 1876, at the age of 16, on the death of his father, Lalique was apprenticed to the celebrated goldsmith Louis Aucoc, whilst simultaneously pursuing his studies at the Ecole des Arts Decoratifs in Paris. Aucoc was a high-priced goldsmith whose wealthy and modish clientele demanded exactly what was fashionable at the time. This was primarily neo-rococo jewellery with heavy and showy cut gems dominating their precious metal settings that was neither technically nor stylistically innovative.

A two year period of study in England, at Sydenham School of Art at Crystal Palace in south London, completed his education, and on his return to France in 1880, he found that the Parisian climate was becoming more sympathetic to the creation of finely crafted objects d'art. In the midst of the machine age, interest had been reawakened to in individual workmanship, an echo of the Arts and

LALIQUE AND JEWELLERY

The jewels of Lalique are among the richest and most telling of all Art Nouveau creations. The myriad brooches, pendants, necklaces, diadems, lorgnettes, hair combs, watch cases and other bijouterie bearing this master's signature comprise a single oeuvre shaped by a vivid imagination and honed by virtuoso technical skills. Lalique's innovative combination of pre-

Crafts Movement that Lalique had witnessed in England.

Lalique worked freelance for the prestigious houses of Cartier, Boucheron, Renn, Gariod, Hamelin and Destape. By 1885 he had taken over Destape's workshop and in the following five years, had expanded the premises. Although he had been exhibiting his jewels as early as the Exposition of 1889, (anonymously, under the names of the large companies for which he was freelancing) it was not until the Paris Salon of 1894 that Lalique displayed his work under his own name. Immediately, he won lavish praise and gained numerous commissions from the 'grandes dames' of the Third Empire. Lalique was well on his way to becoming the most prominent master in his field.

Having opened his own firm, Lalique was free to design jewellery as he wanted, without any restrictions from employers or clients. His designs, which were regularly reproduced in the trade magazine *Le Bijou*, inspired both praise and imitation from numerous colleagues including Alphonse Fouquet and his son, Georges, who took over his father's firm in 1895 and became a well-known Art Nouveau jeweller.

SARAH BERNHARDT

By this time Lalique had already begun to design jewels for his most famous female client, the actress Sarah Bernhardt, and it was she who provided Lalique with the opportunity to apply his talent to relatively large-scale, often audacious, pieces that could be easily seen by the theatre audiences she performed to. Bernhardt commissioned luxurious diadems, necklaces, belts and other stage 'props' which he tailored perfectly to the roles she was playing, such as the Theodora crown of 1884, and

parures for the parts of Gismonda and Iseyl.

Despite the boldness of his theatrical extravagances, Lalique's ruling notion was that a jewel worn by a woman should contribute to the harmony and total effect of her entire ensemble. The stage pieces for Bernhardt and the 140 or so 'museum-pieces' designed for the collector Calouste Gulbenkian, which were never intended to be worn, were exceptions

Above: Lalique pendant brooch in diamond and tourmaline offset by rich plique-a-jour *enamel.*

Right: Lalique's studies for pendants and brooches of dragonflies and butterflies as decorative devices.

Below: A medallion by Lalique of the actress Sarah Bernhardt, c.1900.

to this rule, and they were outnumbered by hundreds of subtler, though no less striking, pieces of bijouterie he produced.

OFFICIAL RECOGNITION

Throughout his three decades as a goldsmith, Lalique continually experimented with new materials and new techniques. He used horn in place of tortoiseshell and elevated that material to a near-luxury status; he employed embroidery techniques on metals, and applied enamels to a variety of surfaces. As his reputation grew, his rebellion against the more usual proliferation of diamonds in joaillerie came to be officially approved by the board of jewellers. By order of the Chambre Syndicale de la Bijouterie de Paris, the use of precious stones or materials alongside semi-precious or 'vulgar' stones and materials was officially sanctioned for the first time.

Without a doubt, the Exposition Universelle of 1900 in Paris, which welcomed the dawn of the new century and commemorated the 30th anniversary of the Third Republic with displays of recent technological achieve-

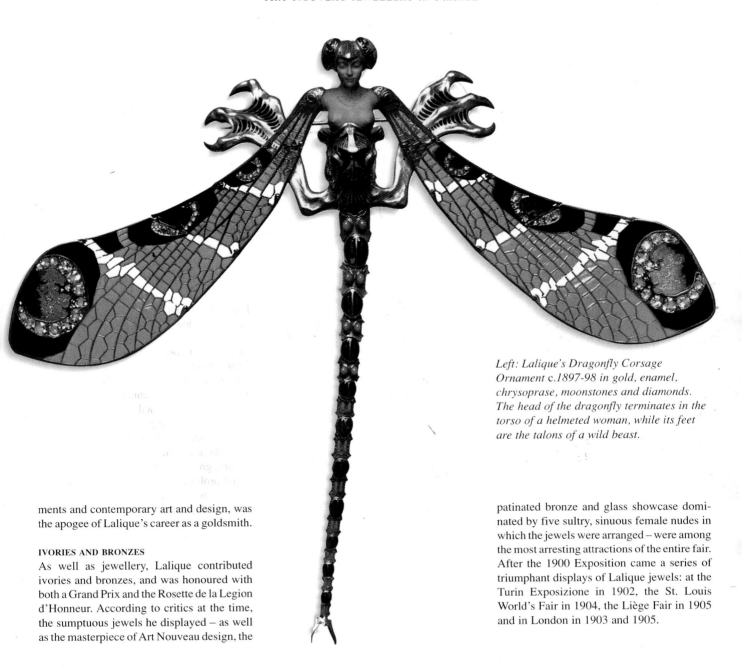

Left: Lalique's Dragonfly Corsage Ornament c.1897-98 in gold, enamel, chrysoprase, moonstones and diamonds. The head of the dragonfly terminates in the torso of a helmeted woman, while its feet are the talons of a wild beast.

ments and contemporary art and design, was the apogee of Lalique's career as a goldsmith.

IVORIES AND BRONZES

As well as jewellery, Lalique contributed ivories and bronzes, and was honoured with both a Grand Prix and the Rosette de la Legion d'Honneur. According to critics at the time, the sumptuous jewels he displayed – as well as the masterpiece of Art Nouveau design, the

patinated bronze and glass showcase dominated by five sultry, sinuous female nudes in which the jewels were arranged – were among the most arresting attractions of the entire fair. After the 1900 Exposition came a series of triumphant displays of Lalique jewels: at the Turin Exposizione in 1902, the St. Louis World's Fair in 1904, the Liège Fair in 1905 and in London in 1903 and 1905.

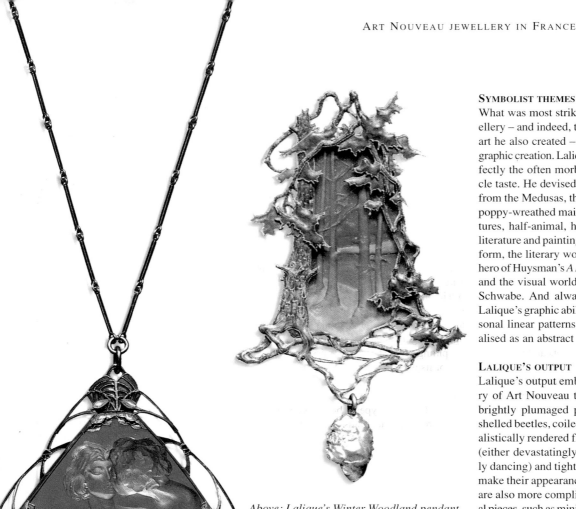

Above: Lalique's Winter Woodland pendant from 1899-1900. Several of Lalique's jewels depict miniature landscapes in great detail.

Left: Lalique's 'The Kiss' pendant, 1904-05. Similar kissing couples appear on other works.

SYMBOLIST THEMES

What was most striking about Lalique's jewellery – and indeed, the multi-media works of art he also created – was the fertility of their graphic creation. Lalique's motifs reflected perfectly the often morbid aspects of fin-de-siècle taste. He devised refined, graphic designs from the Medusas, the Ophelias, the drugged, poppy-wreathed maidens, the grotesque creatures, half-animal, half-human, of symbolist literature and painting. He froze into jewellery form, the literary world of Des Esseintes, the hero of Huysman's *A Rebours* (Against Nature) and the visual world of Khnopff, Redon and Schwabe. And always, whatever the motif, Lalique's graphic ability created distinctly personal linear patterns that could also be visualised as an abstract art in themselves.

LALIQUE'S OUTPUT

Lalique's output embraces the entire repertory of Art Nouveau themes and inspirations: brightly plumaged peacocks and glistening shelled beetles, coiled enamelled serpents, realistically rendered flowers and trees, women (either devastatingly devouring or innocently dancing) and tightly embracing couples all make their appearance in his jewellery. There are also more complicated, multi-dimensional pieces, such as miniature wooded landscapes fashioned from gold, enamel, opals and brilliants which could be attached to a collar; or an ivory carved pendant of a horseman whose steed tramples a nude below, with the entire scene surrounded by three equine heads with stylised manes. Like many of the painters of the second half of the 19th century, such as Whistler, Klimt and some of the Pre-Raphaelites, Lalique created both the work of art and the frame enclosing it, a concept that was revolutionary in the goldsmith's art.

MOTIFS FROM NATURE

The subjects Lalique chose for his bijouterie mostly came from nature. At a young age he had been a shrewd observer of flowers, trees and animals in all their guises and stages of growth. Lalique's floral vocabulary is perhaps his richest, and in the main, the most faithful to nature. Works ranged from a simple hat-pin consisting of three silver birch leaves in horn, their gold seed cones enamelled in a complementary autumnal hue, to a bracelet of five, bluish-violet champlevé enamel irises on gold, all on a carved opal background, as well as a lovely diadem in the shape of an apple tree branch which, but for its composition of horn, gold and diamonds, might just have fallen from the tree.

Flowers and other plant forms are displayed on various brooches, bracelets and pendants, though more often than not, these also incorporate insect or other animal life. The animals Lalique depicted in his jewels spanned nearly all the species of the zoological kingdom from grass hoppers to polar bears, to mythical dragons, sphinxes and bizarre hybrid beasts. Insects, amphibians, reptiles, birds and mammals were all subject to his scrutiny and his craftsman's technique. There was a decided emphasis on creatures favoured by all Art Nouveau designers: the curvilinear swan, seahorse and snake; the brilliantly hued butterflies, peacocks and beetles, as well as more fearful creatures of the night, like bats and serpents.

The snake is one of the strongest subjects in Lalique's Art Nouveau repertory, and the masterpiece among his 'serpent jewels' is the Knot of Serpents pectoral from 1898 comprising nine interlacing snakes whose silver-gilt champlevé enamel bodies of blue, green and black fan out from a top knot, their jaws agape. Originally, each serpent was represented as spitting a row of baroque (misshapen) pearls out of its mouth.

BIRDS

Birds of various types - but especially peacocks, roosters and swans - figure in Lalique's

Above: A thistle-inspired pendant by René Lalique.

Below: Rose branches corsage ornament by René Lalique in gold, glass, amethyst and enamel.

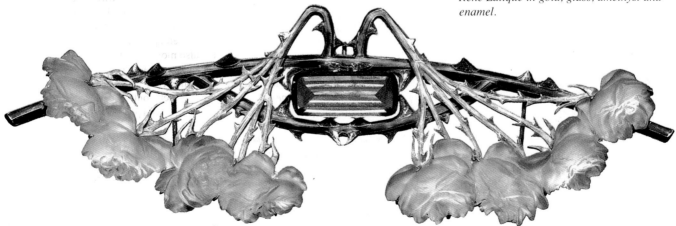

Above: The Knot of Serpents corsage ornament, the masterpiece among Lalique's jewels.

jewellery designs as they do in his glass. One of his best known jewels (and perhaps one of the most unwieldy) is the diadem in the shape of a cock's head. Never before in western art and design had such a lowly barnyard fowl been treated so luxuriantly. The cock's golden beak grasps an amethyst and its open-work gold and enamel comb is as delicately wrought as a spider's web. The cock motif was one that Lalique obviously found interesting for it also appears on a belt buckle. Here two cock's heads in enamelled copper are placed in profile, beak-to-beak.

The peacock had been a motif popular with artists from the Aesthetic Movement such as Whistler, but designers such as Morris and Tiffany chose to depict only its brilliantly hued feathers, often to the point of near abstraction. Lalique however, was eager to display the bird in all its glory. He created a stunning chest ornament in which the bird's enamel and gold tail feathers, richly studded with opals, swirls around its body in a bow-like pattern.

FEMALE FIGURES

The figure of woman also stands out in Lalique's work. Indeed it is she, almost to the total exclusion of the male sex, that dominates Art Nouveau. She appears as the long-haired seductress or the flower-crowned innocent. Lalique is believed to be the first goldsmith since the 16th century to represent the female nude in jewellery, and he did so frequently. He carved them in ivory and coupled them in erotic dances; he veiled them in vines and blossoms and he represented them as shameless pagan nymphs sometimes paired with birds and beasts, and even, the occasional male figure!

Lalique's female figures are not always nude: there is Ophelia reclining under a wil-

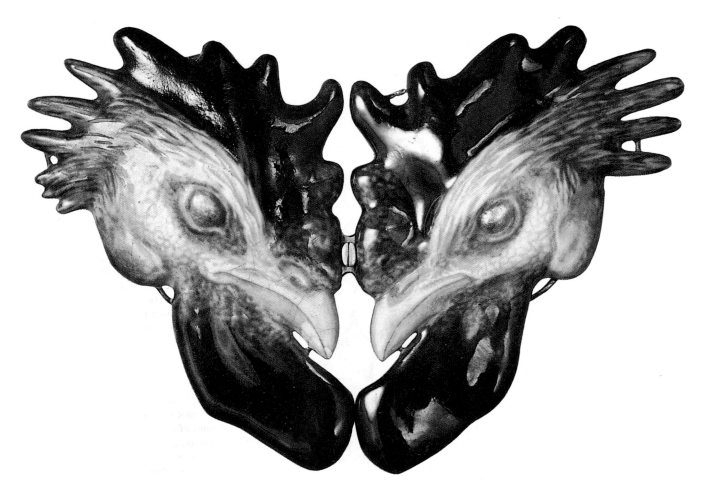

low tree, angels deep in prayer, regal women with strongly carved profiles, Breton peasants in traditional costume. And even when he does not depict women directly, her spirit is often present, for the animals, plants and flowers he used were often Symbolist allegories of woman in her various guises.

LITERARY INFLUENCES

On occasion Lalique interpreted literary characters. The Owls bracelet from around 1900 was inspired by the poem 'Les Hiboux' from *Les Fleurs du Mal* (The Flowers of Evil) by the Dandy-poet Charles Baudelaire. Along a five part gold frieze, four moulded frosted-glass

Above: A belt buckle in the form of two cockerel's heads by Lalique. Enamel on copper and gold clasp, c.1900.

owls, symbols of darkness and the night, are perched among pine cones and branches. A collar of 16 strands of tiny pearls surrounding a central rectangular plaque that features a profile of a smiling young woman, may well tell the story of the Frog Prince, for her head is crowned with a huge green enamel frog, while a host of frogs fill the open work field surrounding her. Most of Lalique's creatures are, however, without specific literary allusion and can be appreciated for their sheer beauty, the delicacy of their execution and the imaginative way in which the elements are arranged.

Below: A bracelet with figures of women in intaglio-moulded glass, diamonds, gold and enamel by Lalique c.1895.

Bottom: The Owls Bracelet by Lalique c. 1900-01, inspired by Charles Baudelaire's poem, 'Les Hiboux'.

JAPONISME

The combs, diadems and other hair ornaments that Lalique produced, mostly of horn embellished with gold, enamel, ivory, glass and stones, are the most realistically nature-laden of his works. In these designs, Lalique was strongly influenced by the irregular design system of flowers which characterised japonisme. The borrowed Oriental style was, thanks to Samuel Bing's efforts in bringing it to public attention, in vogue at the turn of the century.

GULBENKIAN COLLECTION

One comb in the Gulbenkian collection, Wisteria, exhibits a device often used by Lalique: certain carved areas are left 'blank', that is, in their original hued state, whereas other primary areas are built up or emphasised by means of vividly coloured enamels. One of the most obvious borrowings from Japanese art is a necklace from 1890 made of nine spherical *ojime* in ochre lacquer carved with a stylised wave motif and embellished with mother-of-pearl insets. *Ojime* are part of the traditional Japanese costume and are bell-shaped toggles which separate the little seal container-called *inro* from the carved *netsuke*

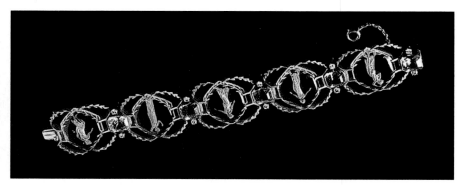

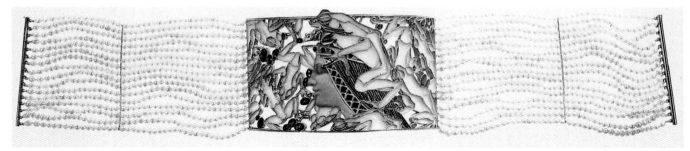

Above: Dog collar depicting the 'Frog Prince' in gold, enamel, glass and pearls by Lalique, c.1900.

Right: A delicately enamelled dragonfly hairpiece by Lalique set against a pendant by Philippe Wolfers.

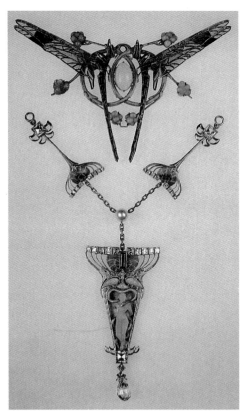

from which it hangs. In Lalique's piece, the *ojime* beads alternate with 20 pairs of dark green enamelled twisted links. Noteworthy not only for its obvious borrowing of Japanese forms, the necklace also translates the common Japanese motif of crested waves into the curvilinear Art Nouveau vocabulary.

GOLD

Looking at the extensive and varied output of Lalique's career as a goldsmith, it is not difficult to understand that there was a talented genius at work. An innovator, arbiter of taste and perfectionist, Lalique the Art Nouveau jeweller was all these and more. But during the years that he was establishing his reputation in bijouterie, Lalique was feeling the pull of another challenge in a material that he had already begun to incorporate into his jewellery, namely, glass. The possibilities for endless shapes, colours and shadings in this material were endless and he was eventually to devote himself fully to its production. Amazingly, after just a few years, the most acclaimed goldsmith at the 1900 Exposition Universelle in Paris was to become the *maître-verrier* of the 20th century.

LALIQUE'S FOLLOWERS

Writing in *Les Modes* in 1901, the critic Roger Marx noted that Lalique had laid open new and unknown possibilities for jewellery, and that the evolution of design in that area owed its sole debt to him. Lalique's work did indeed inspire a number of designers at the turn of the century in Paris. The brothers Paul and Henri Vever and Lucien Gaillard were among the most gifted.

INHERITORS

The Vever brothers were the inheritors of a family business and first attracted attention at the 1900 Exposition Universelle. They exploited the style and the techniques made fashionable by Lalique, and their workshops became particularly adept at enamelling, especially *plique-à-jour* work, where enamel is contained within a framework of metal but has an open back. This allows light to pass through the enamel and the effect is rather like that of a stained-glass window. The Vever brothers acted as entrepreneurs and many of their designs were commission from leading Art Nouveau designers such as Eugene Grasset.and

Edward Colonna, whose jewellery designs, usually asymmetrical creations in silver and gold decorated with enamel and stones, were also sold at Bing's Maison de l'Art Nouveau.

GAILLARD

Lucien Gaillard became director of his family's firm in 1892 and his primary interest was in metalwork. Around 1900, the example of Lalique encouraged him to design jewellery, and despite the evident Lalique influence, Gaillard's jewellery was very successful, winning him first prize at the Societé des Artistes Français in 1904. His most distinctive work is a series of horn hair combs carved as stylised sprays of honesty and mistletoe and often set with small baroque pearls as flower heads or berries.

FOUQUET

Georges Fouquet, who took over his family firm in 1895, was anxious to express himself in the fashionable Art Nouveau idiom, and found an ideal collaborator in the Moravian-born artist, Alphonse Mucha whom Fouquet had commissioned in 1901 to design his new shop in Rue Royale. The combination of Mucha's luscious and refined graphic sense with Fouquet's ability to translate the artist's designs into exquisite works of art produced only a limited number of jewels, but they are amongst the most extraordinary works created in the Art Nouveau period. The major examples of this fruitful collaboration are works of pure fantasy and are jewels of theatrical proportions. Chief among them is the bizarre bracelet conceived for Sarah Bernhardt, a grotesque enamelled and articulated gold griffin which encircles the forearm and hand, and incorporates a ring. There is also a giant *parure de corsage* incorporating a carved ivory head surrounded by carved ivory and gold arabesques of hair, an enamelled halo, pendant baroque stones and a pendant painted panel of water-colour on ivory within a gold border.

Above: Parure de corsage *designed by Alphonse Mucha and made by Georges Fouquet in gold, enamels, emeralds, watercolour and metallic paint on ivory.* c.1900

Left: Brooch by Georges Fouquet from c. 1904.

Far left: A buckle/clasp with grazing stag design by Lalique in glass and metal. c.1908.

LA MAISON MODERNE

Julius Meier-Graef's shop, La Maison Moderne, was one of the outlets that retailed jewellery in high Art Nouveau taste by Paul Follot, Maurice Dufrene and Manuel Orazi, while more traditional firms such as those founded by Frederic Boucheron in 1858, made certain concessions to the fashions of 1900. Designs by L.Hirtz for Boucheron were published in the winter of 1901 in *The Studio* in a special number devoted to jewellery and fans.

EUGÈNE FEUILLATRE

Having mastered the skills of enamelling in Lalique's workshop, Eugène Feuillatre began designing and exhibiting independently. His forte was in large tours-de-force of enamelling including delicate *plique-à-jour* creations of unprecedented daring. The finest surviving example of his work is a 29cm diameter dish, now in the collection of Charles Hadley-Read, the design of which is of a grotesque fish in polychrome enamels within a silver framework.

Left: Horn and gold hair comb by Georges Fouquet.

NON-GALLIC
JEWELLERY

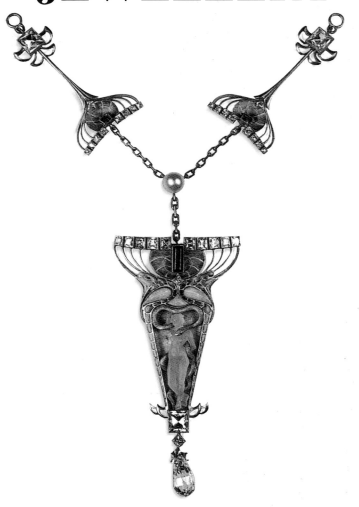

Above: Oxidised silver and cabochon moth pin by C.R Ashbee.

Overleaf: Eve, a pendant designed by Philippe Wolfers in 1901.

The sinuous shapes and striking use of enamels and semiprecious stones gives a distinctive character to the jewellery of the late 19th and early 20th centuries. Beginning with the Art Nouveau period, there was a fundamental change in the attitude towards jewellery in terms both of its design and its function. The aesthetic merits of form, colour and texture became increasingly important, rather than the financial value of the materials used.

Until this period, much of the jewellery made continued the use of precious materials. It was therefore the prerogative of the rich and its role was to demonstrate a person's position in society. When factory production began in earnest in the mid-19th century, many entrepreneurs and industrialists, turned towards the indiscriminate use of ornamentation in order to satisfy the growing consumer market. Even the most mundane and utilitarian of machine-made goods were embellished to make them more desirable to the consumer. This was not a philanthropic exercise. More often it was done to disguise poor workmanship.

Individuals such as John Ruskin and William Morris questioned the effects of large-scale production on art and design. Their followers in the Arts and Crafts Movement of the 1860s were interested in reinstating the aesthetic values of the artist-craftsman in place of those of industrial production.

JEWELLERY IN BRITAIN

At the end of the 19th century, British jewellery differed from that produced in France because it owed more to the traditions established by the Arts and Crafts Movement.

Perhaps the best known of the Arts and Crafts Movement jewellery and metalwork was the product of the Guild of Handicrafts established in 1888 by Charles Robert Ashbee. Ashbee trained as an architect as well as a silversmith and jeweller, and he produced a great many designs in gold, silver, pearls, jade and turquoise, often in the form of that popular motif in Art Nouveau, the peacock. For Ashbee, design was all important, and the gemstones are more often than not, set into the metalwork rather than overwhelming it. The stones themselves reflect the expanding British Empire; the opals are from Australia, the pearls from India, the moonstones from Ceylon and the diamonds from South Africa.

FRED PARTRIDGE

Among the other designers who produced jewellery at the Guild were Fred Partridge, whose work had much in common with the French Art Nouveau designers in his use of horn and steel, and May Hart, a skilled enameller, who later married Partridge.

Enamellers aimed to create a 'people's jewellery' by substituting cheaper glass enamels for gemstones. Moreover, its laws of production appealed to Arts and Crafts idealists: enamel

jewellery was made by at most, three people, in place of a whole team of gem cutters, silversmiths and polishers. To a large extent in Britain, enamelling was also a woman's craft, but one which could be both a hobby and a professional discipline: Phoebe Stabler

Above: Silver, opal and mother-of-pearl peacock brooch designed by C.R. Ashbee.

in Liverpool had in fact studied her craft with a Japanese enameller. Like potters, enamellers generally mastered their craft by trial and error and taught each other new skills.

INFLUENTIAL ENAMELLER

Possibly the most influential enameller in Britain was Alexander Fisher. A former pupil of the French master Dalpayrat, Fisher taught enamelling in his London studio to members of the aristocracy and the leisured middle class. Fisher actively promoted painted enamel as a jewel or art form in its own right. These were either in a single or multiple plaque form, set in gold, silver, bronze, or sometimes even steel, and formed belt buckles, coat clasps, brooches, pendant necklaces and rings which were all designed to be worn with the new, simpler, more 'Rational Dress' fashions of the time. Because it came closest to miniature or easel painting, enamelling gained perhaps the widest acceptance of all the newly revived crafts, and was no doubt encouraged by Fisher's popular instructional book, *The Art of Enamelling on Metal*.

BROMSGROVE GUILD OF APPLIED ART

Other guilds were to flourish in Britain including the Bromsgrove Guild of Applied Art founded in 1890, and the Artificer's Guild of 1891. At Bromsgrove were Joseph Hodel, whose silver buckles, brooches and pendants were in foliate and fruit forms and dotted with semiprecious stones. Arthur Gaskin's jewellery contained cabochon (domed, unfaceted) stones, rope borders, silver or gold filigree wires and clusters of silver beads and tendrils. From 1899, Gaskin worked with his wife, Georgina Cave

Left: A pendant in gold, pearls, amethysts and moonstones by C.R. Ashbee from 1902.

France, an extremely talented craftswoman in jewellery and metals. Mrs. Gaskin had been designing in silver since her student days at the Birmingham School of Art and the Gaskins' pieces are marked with a capital 'G'.

THE ARTIFICER'S GUILD

Members of the Artificer's Guild, founded by Nelson Dawson with his wife Edith, produced work in a number of different media. They also explored the potentials in jewellery of base materials like horn and shell, cloisonné, champlevé and the technically challenging method of unbacked, *plique-à-jour* enamelling.

Other British jewellery designers included the Scottish jeweller based in London Sybil Dunlop, Harold Stabler (a founder member of the Design and Industries Association, the forerunner of the Design Council), Henry Wilson, Omar Ramsden and Alwyn Carr. But possibly the most significant contribution to British Art Nouveau was the jewellery marketed by Arthur Lazenby Liberty.

LIBERTY & CO.

Liberty had opened his shop in 1875, initially specialising in the importing and retailing of Oriental goods from India and Japan. By the turn of the century, its affluent clientele were to include the residents of the new garden cities and suburbs of London. Liberty's stocked one-off, hand-made items as well as factory made goods. Demand was such that the store, while continuing to use independent suppliers, also began to operate its own design studios and manufacturing workshops.

Designers from the Arts and Crafts Movement were employed to create innu-

Right: Enamelled triptych made by Alexander Fisher, c.1900.

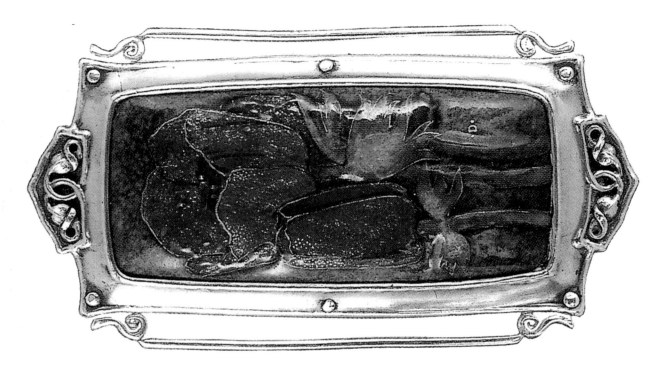

Above: Enamelled silver buckle decorated with a floral motif by the Arts and Crafts jeweller Nelson Dawson, a founder of the Artificer's Guild.

merable products from furniture and textiles, to ceramics and silverware.

CYMRIC AND PEWTER

Liberty sold silveware under the name of 'Cymric' (silver) and 'Tudric' (pewter) from the 1890s. Both these included a large collection of jewellery designed and manufactured by Jessie M. King, Rex Silver, Georgina and Arthur Gaskin, Oliver Baker and Archibald Knox, who created more than 400designs for the firm which were in the main, responsible for defining and determining the 'Liberty style'. Knox had studied Celtic design at the Douglas School of Art on the Isle of Man, and applied the Runic interlacing of forms in his

designs. There is an affinity between the forms used by Alexander Fisher and Knox, but where Fisher used the style by way of decoration, Knox employed the form in a more integral, structural manner.

Initially their designs were made by hand, ,but by the end of the 19th century, jewellery and silverware was increasingly manufactured by machine and contracted out to various firms, including the Birmingham firm of W.H Haseler. They included brooches, pendants, belt buckles and clasps and necklaces. The designers favoured the use of semiprecious stones such as peridot, tourmaline, moonstones and chrysoprase, but in a few instances, precious stones such as rubies, sapphires, emer-

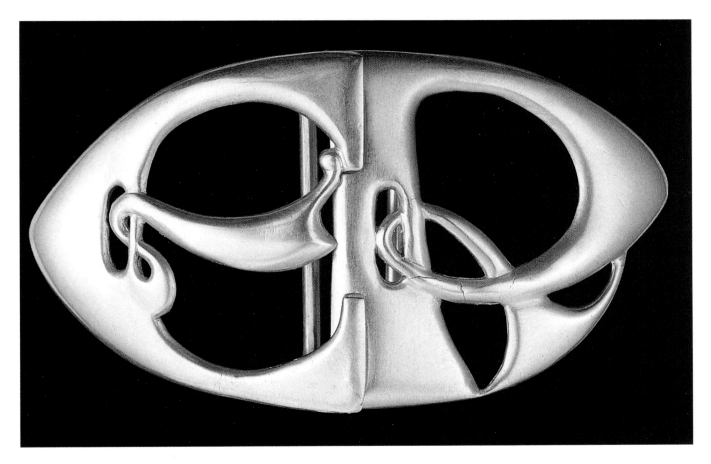

alds, fine pearls and diamonds were used. The use of gems however, was often dependent on the commissions of the purchaser. Often less precious materials were preferred by the designers not just because of cost, but because individual creativity took preference over conforming to traditional aesthetic practices.

DRESS REFORM

The market for such jewellery was however, limited to the more 'enlightened' and artistic of Liberty's clients who appreciated the new aesthetic and moralistic qualities associated with the Arts and Crafts Movement, as well as with the dress reforms of the late 19th century. Dress reform was concerned with removing the restrictions imposed on the body by Victorian costume. In 1881 in Britain, the Rational Dress Society had been formed, which campaigned against the wearing of corsets and

Above: Silver belt buckle designed by Archibald Knox who worked for Liberty & Co in the first decade of the 20th century. This piece has the same stylised abstract quality found in European Art Nouveau.

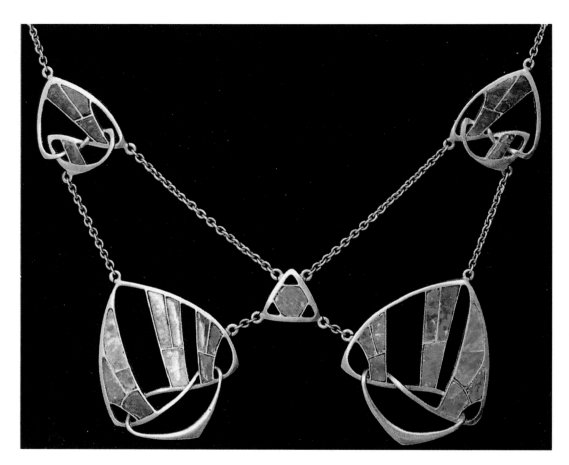

Above: A gold and opal necklace by Archibald Knox for Liberty & Co.

advocated the adoption of looser, simpler garments that could be adorned with large and eye-catching pieces of jewellery, such as a robe clasp. Elsewhere, there were important parallel developments: in Germany the leading critic of contemporary dress was Dr. Gustav Jaeger from Stuttgart who introduced his Sanitary Woollen System in 1878, while in the United States, the American Free Dress Society had been founded.

Advocates of the new, free styles of dress for both men and women included the dancers Loie Fuller and Isadora Duncan, and the novelist and playwright, George Bernard Shaw.

THE GLASGOW FOUR
In Scotland the foremost exponents of Art Nouveau were the 'Glasgow Four', Charles Rennie Mackintosh, his wife, Margaret

Macdonald, her sister Frances, and Frances' husband James Herbert MacNair, who worked independently and together from the 1890s. Each was influenced by the formal organisation and economy of Japanese art and their own Celtic heritage and the elongated, gaunt austerity of their work earned them the name of the 'Spook School'. Their jewellery bore some resemblance to English Arts and Crafts, but its repertory of motifs was very much its own and more in the spirit of Vienna Secession (Austrian Art Nouveau). Among the silver and jewellery designs of the Glasgow Four were stylised birds, leaves, blossoms and hearts.

ART NOUVEAU OUTSIDE BRITAIN

The Arts and Crafts Movement assumed many different guises throughout Europe and America with some significant differences. While the British abhorrence of industrialisation was not shared by many other countries – especially those who had not yet been industrialised and had no reason to reject it – two fundamental aspects of Arts and Crafts ideology were embraced. The first was the use of design to express a country's national identity, and the second, was the attempt to reform design by applying certain Arts and Crafts values to machine production.

Left: A silver and enamel belt buckle designed by Jessie M. King for Liberty & Co in 1906.

OCTOBER, 1902   ONE SHILLING

SCRIBNERS MAGAZINE

Mills Thompson
Del.

CHARLES SCRIBNER'S SONS, NEW YORK. SAMPSON LOW, MARSTON & CO., Ltd., LONDON

THE STUDIO

The two areas most influenced by the ideals of Ruskin, Morris and the other leading lights of the British Arts and Crafts Movement were Scandinavia and the countries in middle Europe, Austria, Hungary and Germany. Their leaders read the works of Ruskin and Morris, subscribed to journals like *The Studio,* and visited Britain and the major international exhibitions to see at first hand the British crafts on display.

SCANDINAVIA

From 1890 onwards,, the Scandinavians were to emerge from being merely imitative in the field of the decorative arts to holding a major position in European design. In some fields and at certain points their influence was to spread beyond their own countries.

These developments were led by Denmark and Sweden, which could build on centuries of independent nationhood and a long established court culture with accompanying high standards of taste and workmanship. No such similar traditions existed in Finland or Norway, however, as both were to gain political and cultural independence only in the early 20th century. The political union between Norway and Sweden was dissolved in 1905 and that between Finland and Russia in 1919.

Returning to their own indigenous folk arts for inspiration, and seeking a naturalistic style to soften the edge of the nascent modernity, the Scandinavian countries drew on the idealised democratic principles of craft production and searched for an aesthetic formula in keeping with their cultural traditions. They

Left: A cover for Scribner's Magazine *by Mills Thompson. Magazines such as these helped spread the Art Nouveau style.*

Left: A silver purse frame with Celtic entrelac motif by Archibald Knox.

Above: A piece by one of the most famous names in Scandinavian design Georg Jensen, known for his abstract forms.

recognised the need to invite industrial sponsorship, not only to maintain links with the market place, but also to provide support for the designers. They hoped that this would eventually lead to the widespread dissemination of well designed and well made goods.

The great name in Scandinavian silver and jewellery was, of course, Georg Jensen, an artist whose fascination with his craft resulted in the creation of some of the most outstanding pieces of silver and jewellery. His

designs betray a remarkable sensitivity to form, while the celebrated, almost matt-hammered finish became an international hallmark of the Jensen style.

AUSTRIA AND THE WIENER WERKSTATTE

In Austria, the search for a new style at the beginning of the 20th century was led by the architect Josef Hoffmann and the members of the Secession group that had been organised as a rebellion against the official *Kunstlerhuas*

(Society of Artists) and its narrow definition of what constituted art. The primary motive of the Secessionists was to bring Austria to the forefront of modern art. Their definition of modern art gave the applied arts equal status to fine arts, but Hoffmann wanted to take the goal of unifying art forms still further. After visiting Ashbee's Guild of Handicraft in 1902, Hoffmann determined to establish a similar craft organisation. In the programme of the *Wiener Werkstätte*, which he founded with fel-

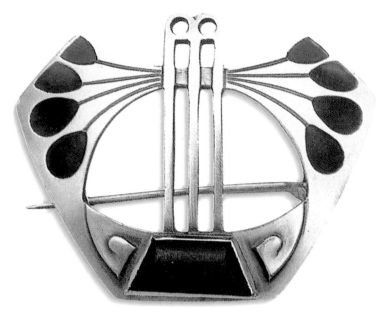

Above right: A later brooch in silver by Georg Jensen.

Above: Scandinavian design during this period was relatively formal as seen in this silver clip by Georg Jensen.

low Secessionist architect Kolomon Moser, Hoffmann declared that their aim was to create an 'island of tranquillity' which amid the 'joyful hum of arts and crafts' would be welcome to followers of Ruskin and Morris.

But Hoffmann was selective in his choice of Arts and Crafts principles. Ignoring the aspects of social reform, Hoffmann adopted only those principles concerned with the reform of design – functionalism and craftsmanship which were most rigorously combined in a reductive geometry of forms. Many historians credit this to the influence of Mackintosh, whose designs were greeted with wild acclaim in Vienna and who was also a close friend of Hoffmann. Regardless of the source of inspiration, the square would become the leitmotif of the *Wiener Werkstätte* designs.

Hoffmann and Moser also championed the use of more modest materials such as semi-precious stones for jewellery in the belief that exceptional design and craftsmanship were more important. Both were passionate about the highest standards of craftsmanship, but, when special commissions were to be undertaken, about the finest materials.

Whether plain and simple, patterned, or highly ornamented, privately commissioned or made in multiples, the products of the *Wiener Werkstätte* were expensive. Although they did not shun the use of machinery, the *Werkstätte* members would not compromise their high ideals of craftsmanship to make good design available to all.

THE CRAFT IN GERMANY

In Germany, the equivalent of Art Nouveau was known as *Jugendstil*, which became the

Above: A selection of jewellery designed by Theodor Fahrner from 1900-1920.

major influence on the decorative arts by 1900. The attitude of the Vienna *Werkstätte* was not one shared by most of the workshops established in Germany.

The first and most influential was the United Workshops for Art and Craftsmanship, founded in 1897 in Munich. While the members of this group looked to the example of Britain and its precedent in raising design standards by applying simplicity, integrity and fitness of purpose to making everyday objects, they rejected the belief held by Ruskin and Morris about the sanctity of the hand-made. Like their Viennese contemporaries, the German group was uninterested in social reform, but they also differed strongly in that the German members were also indifferent to individualism in the work process.

Their aim was to make quality goods at an affordable price, and they supported any methods that would improve the standard of German goods to make them more competitive in the international and domestic market. By employing the latest technologies, the designer worked in close co-operation with the makers and manufacturers, a rejection of the Arts and Crafts idea that the designer was also the maker. In jewellery, designers such as Peter Behrens, Henry Van de Velde, Josef Olbrich, Patriz Huber and Carl Otto Czechka contributed designs for mass production by the firm of Theodor Farhner in Pforzheim, the centre of the German jewellery industry between 1900 and 1930.

JEWELLERY IN AMERICA

The Arts and Crafts reformers' designs were shaped by moral convictions and often prescribed how people should live. The moral aesthetics of American reformers were once again developed from the works of Ruskin

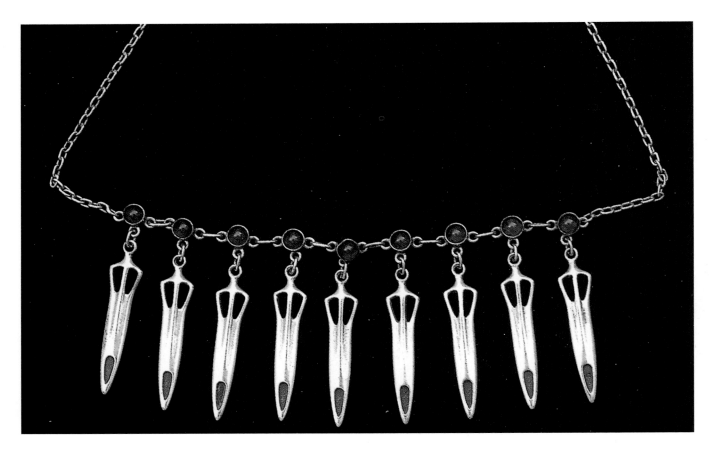

Above: Silver and amethyst necklace inspired by the rectilinear qualities of Art Nouveau. It was manufactured in 1905 by the firm of Theodor Fahrner in Pforzheim, the centre of the German jewellery industry.

and Morris whose writings were best sellers in America. Between 1859 and 1892, for example, Ruskin's only book devoted to the decorative arts, *The Two Paths*, was reprinted 19 times and many reading groups were established across the country to study the works of other writers. Joseph Twyman established a William Morris room in the Tobey Furniture Company of Chicago's showrooms and also founded a William Morris Society.

Although Morris and Ruskin never visited the United States, many other leaders of the British Arts and Crafts Movement made the journey. Among them were Walter Crane, Charles Ashbee and Morris's daughter May, and all gave lectures and toured exhibitions of their work.

ELIZABETH E. COPELAND
Inspired by the movement, many individuals and groups in America followed the British lead and turned to the professional practice of their crafts. In Boston, where the Arts and

Crafts first took hold in America, Elizabeth E. Copeland, after studying in England, combined silver and enamel in her work which clearly showed the handicraft of the maker. Following her, Edward Everette Oakes, also in Boston, designed jewellery and showed at the Arts and Crafts Society's Exhibition in 1923. In Chicago, Florence Koehler made jewellery in the Art Nouveau style that owed a stylistic debt more to France than England.

MADELINE YALE WYNNE

During this period, *The Craftsman* magazine extolled the virtues of simplicity and practicality, and while the latter virtue is always questionable in relation to jewellery, these beliefs were to influence the works of artist-jewellers like Madeline Yale Wynne. Wynne explored the artistic potential of different non-precious materials such as copper, pebbles and rock crystals. This would prove to be a more enduring influence on future jewellery design than those companies and individuals preoccupied with precious metals and stones, since the search for new forms indirectly reflected the modern world. Other American jewellers who practised within the Arts and Crafts arena include Brainerd Bliss Thresher and Josephine Hartwell

One name, however, that stands out in the design and manufacture of Art Nouveau jewellery in America is that of Tiffany & Co. which produced a prolific amount of jewellery from the latter half of the 19th century, at first inspired by British Arts and Crafts, and later by Continental Art Nouveau in the first decade

Below: A Swordfish brooch manufactured by Tiffany's during the 1930s in diamonds, sapphires, emeralds and rubies.

of the 20th century.

Louis Comfort Tiffany, famous for his masterpieces in glass, had been trained as an painter. Louis' father Charles had amassed an enormous store of precious stones over the years and his craftsmen used them in designs for sword scabbards, tiaras and coronets. In collaboration with Julia Munson, Louis opened an 'art jewellery' department in the store and oversaw the production of luxurious Byzantine-inspired designs, utilising such materials as opals and amethysts, rubies, diamonds and emeralds. Jewellery designed by Louis Comfort Tiffany was produced under the auspices of Tiffany & Co. and bore their mark, so verification of Louis' own designs is difficult.

TIFFANY'S JEWELLERY

What distinguishes Tiffany's jewellery from it European counterparts is that Tiffany did not make the gemstones subordinate to their settings, preferring instead a hard, clear design with unobtrusive settings. These pieces were perhaps too expensive and the 'art jewellery' department closed in 1916, although the company of Tiffany & Co. continued to produce fine jewellery.

Left: Tiffany mixed opals with translucent glass in this necklace, but unlike his contemporaries, he did not submerge the gemstones in their settings.

ART NOUVEAU
METALWORK

Overleaf: Silver mounted jug by C. R Ashbee at the Guild of Handicrafts, c.1900. The green glass was made by Powell's of Whitefriars.

Below: The gate of Horta's Van Eetvelde House, whose intricate curving style is repeated inside.

The mid-19th century witnessed the beginnings of an age of individuality and innovation in terms of both precious and non-precious metalwork. The standards of Art Nouveau craftsmanship in this area were extremely high, and the period was rich in its constant variety of invention. Since the essence of Art Nouveau was the curving, sinuous line, its insubstantiality was best exploited in malleable materials.

ART NOUVEAU METAL IN ARCHITECTURE

Metal, particularly wrought-iron was a significant part of Art Nouveau architecture, both structurally and decoratively. Victor Horta had made its structural role clear in his work in Brussels and he had also used it decoratively, exploiting its relative malleability to provide lighter patterns in contrast to the weightiness of stone. In Art Nouveau architecture, metalwork serves as a link between the building itself and the style of its contents, which were often the product of the same designer. From exterior balconies, gates and window mullions, the metal is continued into the interior in columns, beams, banisters and door handles, and even to embellishments on furniture.

The versatile applications for metalwork and the range of metals available encouraged almost every Art Nouveau architect and interior designer to turn their hand to metal at some stage. As with glass or furniture, it is important to visualise metalwork as part of its context in the interior scheme. It could appear in the form of candlesticks, flatware, clocks, light fittings, mirrors, caskets and in fanciful, decorative sculptures.

EXTERIORS AND INTERIORS

Hector Guimard's Métro entrances emphasise the versatility of the medium, as they can be seen both as architecture and as sculpture, or even as enormous decorative pieces. They use

Above: The whiplash line, is evident in Guimard's ironwork entrance to the Castel Beranger.

Left: The Paris Metro, Bois de Boulogne station by Hector Guimard, who also designed the typography.

the same forms as the great iron gates of the Castel Beranger apartments, as well as for the banisters within. In Belgium, Horta carried the same continuity of form from the iron balconies to the banisters for the staircase, the main feature of his own home and studio in the Rue Americaine in Brussels.

Comparable in function, yet even more fantastic in form, were the balconies of Gaudi's Casa Mila, modelled like tangled seaweed. In his early work for the Casa Vicens, Gaudi achieved the effect of palm fronds with the spikes cut at the top bent in every direction as if they were dropping leaves. The entrance gate to the Guell Estate in Pedrables is even more outstanding. Here, almost the entire piece is treated in the form of a writhing dragon whose gaping jaw reaches out to ensnare the hand of the visitor who reaches for the handle.

METAL OBJECTS D'ART
Work in the traditional precious metals, particularly silver, had, through the processes of industrialisation and mass production, sunk

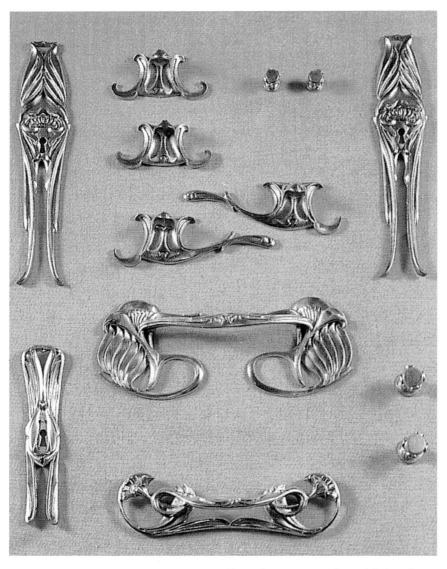

Above: An ornate set of metal fittings for furniture produced by Georges de Feure.

to a low level of design and workmanship until it was revived by the Arts and Crafts Movements, first in England and then later abroad.

These craftsmen emphasised the virtues of handmade objects, and at times even sought to underline this method of production by deliberately leaving the surface of their metal objects 'unfinished' — that is, with their hammer marks left visible and unpolished. Less precious materials were also explored for their aesthetic qualities: bronze, brass, tin and copper were all used, and a revival of interest in pewter also occurred. At times, Art Nouveau craftsmen combined a range of metals and mixed them with ivory, enamels, semiprecious stones or any other material required to produce the appropriate effect. Some designers produced handmade and therefore very exclusive items, while others were to tailor their designs to large-scale production and found themselves more in tune with the future course of design in the 20th century.

ART NOUVEAU METALWORK IN FRANCE

Guimard was largely an isolated talent in France with regard to architectural metalwork, and the French reputation in metalwork is largely confined to the area of jewellery and orfeverie. In France, the Nancy school concentrated more on furniture, glass and ceramics, although Louis Majorelle, who had used gilt trimmings on his furniture, produced some gates and banisters, as did Victor Prouve. More metalwork was produced by the Parisian craftsmen working for Bing, and Julius Meier-Graefe, who had opened his retail outlet La Maison Moderne in Paris in 1898. The elegant Georges de Feure was one of the most versatile of these designers and produced objects from candelabra to walking cane handles, based on stylised, fluid plant forms. Others, like Colonna and Selmersheim, turned to metalwork for a complete room setting, designing table-lamps or chandeliers in the form of drooping plants whose flowers were the glass shades.

CARDEILHAC

The firm of Cardeilhac was a leading producer of exciting Art Nouveau designs, in particular by Lucien Bonvallet. The company also produced a series of mounts for vases by the leading glass makers and potters, and the firm's most characteristic pieces were those in silver or silver-gilt, decorated with stylised yet restrained plant motifs.

Like many Art Nouveau designers, Lucien Gaillard, a name most often associated with jewellery, also explored a range of media. Gaillard had studied in depth the various aspects of metal working, patination, plating and alloying, as well as Japanese techniques of decoration. He produced a variety of objects from parasol handles to hairpins which combined his fine workmanship with a strong sense of design, using precious and non-precious materials with equal respect.

SCULPTURE IN METAL

Another branch of the decorative arts which enjoyed a particular vogue at the end of the 19th century was decorative sculpture. Small, domestic scale sculptures could be found in a variety of functions, including supporting lamps, as well as being created in a purely ornamental capacity. This was principally a French-inspired fashion pursued by such figures as Eugène Feuillatre, Raoul Larche, Théodore Rivière and Rupert Carabin, who generally produced nude or lightly-draped female figures whose hair and drapery was ex-

Left: Decorative sculpture enjoyed a particular vogue around 1900. One of the most popular motifs of the Art Nouveau period was the figure of a woman as the 'dream-maiden'.

tended into extravagant arabesques.

French sculpture at the time was dominated by the ageing genius, Auguste Rodin, whose work, principally in bronze, had exploited to the full that medium's possibilities for active poses and shimmering light. Rodin's work however, was far too involved with symbolist and literary overtones to be described as decorative, yet his frequently twisting poses and erotic subjects do recall some aspects of Art Nouveau.

FOLIES BERGÈRE
The main source of inspiration for Art Nouveau sculptors was undoubtedly the American dancer, Loie Fuller, who first appeared at the Folies Bergère in 1893, and triumphed at the 1900 Exposition Universelle where she was hailed as the living embodiment of Art Nouveau. Several sculptors captured the fluid magic of her dance movements in bronze.

MAURICE BOUVAL
Some of the most sensual decorative Art Nouveau sculptures were modelled by Maurice Bouval. His works, which were conceived as paper knives, dishes, door handles or purely decorative objects, were usually in gilt-bronze and always on the theme of the dream-maiden or femme-fleur (woman-flower) so dear to Art Nouveau. A regional variant of this genre was produced in Belgium by the jeweller Philippe Wolfres, who in 1904, devoted himself entirely to this form of decorative sculpture.

Sculptor and decorator Albert Charpentier

Left: Gilt and silver-bronze statuette by E Barrias called 'La Naturese devoilant devant La Science'.

modelled low relief, sensitive allegorical nude figures for door handles, furniture decorations and lock plates, and was regarded as one of the best medallists during his active period at the turn of the century.

SIR ALFRED GILBERT

The British sculptor Sir Alfred Gilbert, the creator of the Shaftesbury Memorial fountain at Piccadilly in London, (better known as 'Eros') was a sculptor in bronze who changed to working on a smaller scale with precious and semi-precious materials. In the detailing of his works – even those on a large scale – Gilbert was fascinated by intricate, twisting and curving forms, often tinged with marine mythology taken from the 16th and 17th centuries.

METALWORK IN ENGLAND

Silver was one of the materials which had received renewed attention due to the influence of the Arts and Crafts Movement. Silver design largely transferred from the established manufacturers to artists and architects who turned their hand to silversmithing. Perhaps the best known of the Arts and Crafts metalwork designers is Charles Ashbee, who had founded the Guild of Handicrafts in 1888. Ashbee began working in silver and electroplate in 1889, although did he not register a mark until 1896. The first works produced by the Guild were in keeping with their high ideals. They avoided the abhorred smooth, mechanical finish produced by high polishing. Instead, Ashbee encouraged his craftsmen to leave the impression of hammer marks on the surface of their work. From 1890 the Guild began using gems and enamelling, but

Right: Gilt bronze 'femme-fleur' bust by Maurice Bouval, c.1900.

Right: 'Comedy and Tragedy' by Sir Alfred Gilbert. The fluid lines connect it with decorative elements of Art Nouveau.

Ashbee's work is most recognisable from his wirework, which he perfected around 1897, and the delicacy of his designs which often incorporate green glass with silver.

With regard to design for industrial manufacture, it is the work of Christopher Dresser that represents the highest achievement. Dresser based his design ethic on 'fitness for purpose' and most of them were carried out in electroplate, due as much to his concern for an economic use of materials as to the manufacturer's financial preference. One of the few designers to have visited Japan, Dresser's metalwork designs demonstrate a sparseness and in some cases, a complete lack of decoration which is in complete contrast to many of the other leading Art Nouveau designers.

LIBERTY STYLE

Liberty & Co. was one of the leading English retailers of metalwork in the Art Nouveau style. Designs for silver and metalwork were commissioned from various designers, including Rex Silver, Oliver Baker, Bernard Cuzner, Arthur Gaskin and Jessie M. King. The most outstanding of Liberty's designers, and the one who would largely determine the Liberty style was Archibald Knox. Born on the Isle of Man, Knox had studied at first hand the Celtic design of the area's cultural history and applied the Runic interlacing of forms in his designs for silver and pewter. In 1899 Liberty's marketed the designs in silver under the vaguely Celtic name of 'Cymric'. At this time Liberty's had stocked German pewter wares but in 1903, following the success of Cymric silver, the store launched its range of 'Tudric' pewter, again, designed largely by Knox.

THE GLASGOW FOUR

A similar mood was created by the work of

the 'Glasgow Four' which centred around the architect and designer Charles Rennie Mackintosh. The two sisters, Margaret and Frances Macdonald produced together and individually, a great deal of relief work, either of beaten tin or silver, as mounts for objects such as mirrors and as decorative objects in their own right. The pale coolness of their work perfectly complements the Mackintosh interior and adds a figurative and floral element to the Glasgow style.

GERMANY AND AUSTRIA

The majority of the members of the main German and Austrian Secessionist groups worked in both precious and base metals. The *Wiener Werkstätte*'s metalwork was made in an extraordinary range of styles, something that was particularly true of Joseph Hoffmann's designs. The earliest examples, dating from 1903, are often very formal, with simple 'modernist' shapes, and in some instance these pieces were left with a hammered finish. Pieces such as the silver-gilt tea service designed in 1904 rank among the greatest metalwork of the period.

INSPIRATION

Much of the early work of both Hoffmann and Kolomon Moser shows the obvious influence of Mackintosh, Ashbee and Henry van de Velde. Highly respected by the Vienna Secessionists, Mackintosh's influence can be seen in the strongly geometric, open lattice-work baskets designed by Hoffmann, while Ashbee's work inspired some of Hoffmann's flattened, covered dishes which date from around 1908.

Below: A silver bowl with wirework handles by C.R Ashbee of the Guild of Handicrafts.

Right: A candlestick in painted copper, brass and wood by Christopher Dresser made by Perry & Co. in 1883.

Below: A teapot by Christopher Dresser in silver and wood from 1881.

In Germany there was a great deal of very ornate Art Nouveau metalwork, especially that produced by firms such as J. P. Kayser Sohne of Krefeld who manufactured a range of pewter under the trade name of Kayser-Zinn. It was this pewter range, designed by Hugo Leven, that Liberty's in London sold until it developed its own Tudric pewter. WMF in Geislingen produced some of the most outrageous curvilinear Art Nouveau metalwork, usually in thick pewter or nickel-silver and often with green glass liners. On of the largest and most important firms was P. Bruckmann & Sohne of Heilbronn, whose designers included Peter Behrens, Friedrich Adler, George Roehmer and Bernhard Wenig. Bruckmann

Above: A teaset of almost oriental refinement by Christopher Dresser.

Left: Teaset by Archibald Knox for Liberty & Co, part of the Tudric range he designed which continued the Celtic theme.

was also one of the major industrial firms to produce the designs of the *Deutsche Werkbund*.

HENRY VAN DE VELDE
Possibly the most impressive of the metalwork designers active in Germany in the early years of the 20th century was Henry van de Velde. His early silver is in a style that is often described as 'geometric-curvilinear' and can be compared to some of the earliest designs by the Dane, Georg Jensen.

OTHER EUROPEAN COUNTRIES
Italian-born designer Carlo Bugatti created both outstanding furniture and magnificent silver objects which were made by the Parisian craftsman Adrien A. Hebrard. In true Art Nouveau style, they combined various subjects, materials and techniques in an unusual manner. For example, one tea and coffee service comprised a long tray with a bizarre animal head at each end, both terminating in long, ivory tusks. The coffee pot, teapot, creamer and sugar bowl were also in the shape of boar-like animal heads, also with ivory tusks.

In St. Petersburg, master jeweller Peter Carl Fabergé included Art Nouveau pieces in his outstanding oeuvre, including gold cigarette cases and flower- and leaf-shaped mounts for the glass made by Tiffany in New York and Loetz in Germany.

METAL IN AMERICA
On the whole, silver in America had tended to be dominated by the old established firms such as the Gorham Manufacturing Co., or the internationally famous, Tiffany and Co.

Left: A jewellery box designed by Charles Rennie Mackintosh.

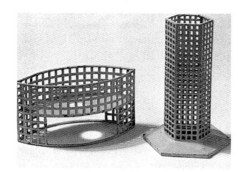

Left: Metal baskets designed by Josef Hoffmann, the founder of the Weiner Werkstatte.

Below: An electric kettle designed by Peter Behrens for AEG c. 1908.

At the luxury end of the market these two firms were the dominant force, and both were influenced by the changes in style created by the craft revival and Art Nouveau.

TIFFANY & CO

Tiffany & Co. the New York jeweller, silver manufacturer and retailer was established in 1837 and it produced outstanding silver in Japanese, Indian and Moorish styles, and, from the 1880s, in the Art Nouveau style. When Louis Comfort Tiffany opened his own Tiffany Studios, he began experimenting with enamels, often used on repousse copper bowls or vases. Opaque and translucent layers were used, fired separately and often finished with an iridescent coat which gave the pieces an effect similar to his glassware.

GORHAM MANUFACTURING COMPANY

The Gorham Manufacturing Company, founded in 1831, in Providence, Rhode Island, was Tiffany's chief rival in silverware, and also produced electroplated silver. In the late 1880s, its fine quality silver included Japanese- style wares and later, hand-crafted pieces in the French Art Nouveau and English Arts and Crafts style which were marketed as 'Martele' (hammered) silver.

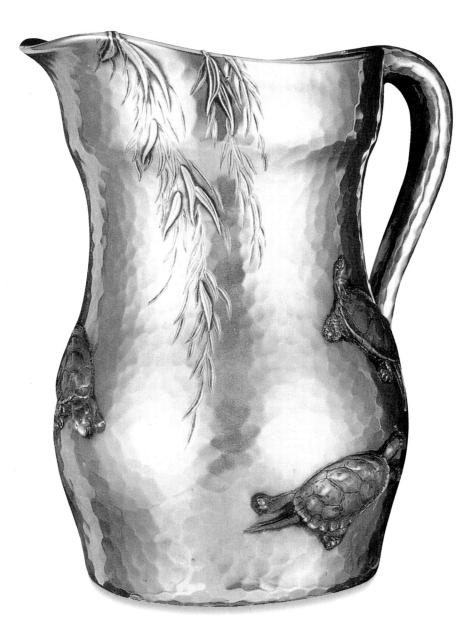

The Arts and Crafts Movement inspired numerous followers in America and several communities fostered a revival in metalwork. The Roycrofters made wrought iron, and the Roycroft Copper Shop was headed by Karl Kipp from Vienna. Kipp designed bookends, candlesticks, trays, vases and other household items which were then made by other members of the Shop. The hammered copper was decorated with stylised designs, usually of flowers or trees and was advertised and sold through the Roycroft catalogues.

Left: Silver, silver gilt and copper jug, decorated with hammered turtles by Tiffany & Company, late 19th century.

Below: A hammered bowl with the same applied turtles, typical of Tiffany's Japanese-style wares.

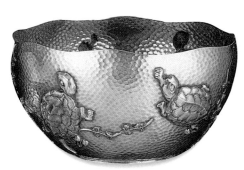